BEES·DANCE
AND·WHALES·SING

Fireflies use their lights to send mating signals

BEES·DANCE AND·WHALES·SING

The Mysteries of Animal Communication

BY MARGERY FACKLAM

ILLUSTRATIONS BY PAMELA JOHNSON

SIERRA CLUB BOOKS FOR CHILDREN

San Francisco

This book is for Alex Paul Facklam

The Sierra Club, founded in 1892 by John Muir, has devoted itself to the study and protection of the earth's scenic and ecological resources—mountains, wetlands, woodlands, wild shores and rivers, deserts and plains. The publishing program of the Sierra Club offers books to the public as a nonprofit educational service in the hope that they may enlarge the public's understanding of the Club's basic concerns. The Sierra Club has some sixty chapters in the United States and in Canada. For information about how you may participate in its programs to preserve wilderness and the quality of life, please address inquiries to Sierra Club, 730 Polk Street, San Francisco, CA 94109.

A LUCAS • EVANS BOOK

Text Copyright © 1992 by Margery Facklam
Illustrations copyright © 1992 by Pamela Johnson

First Edition

Library of Congress Cataloging-in-Publication Data

Facklam, Margery.
   Bees dance and whales sing: the mysteries of animal communication/by Margery Facklam; illustrations by Pamela Johnson.
      p.   cm.
   Includes index.
   Summary: Explores the mysteries of how and why animals send messages to one another and to humans.
   ISBN 0-87156-573-0
   1. Animal communication — Juvenile literature. [1. Animal communication.] I. Johnson, Pamela, ill. II. Title.
QL776.F33   1992
591.59—dc20   91-40556
Printed in the United States of America

10 9 8 7 6 5 4 3 2 1

CONTENTS

1
MAGIC MARKERS
AND SECRET SIGNALS

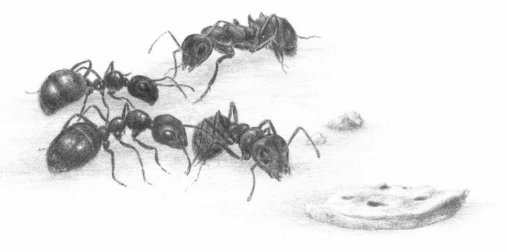

Fire ants follow a chemical trail

"Don't drop crumbs on the floor," you've probably been told. "Crumbs attract ants."

It certainly seems that way. If one ant finds cookie crumbs on the kitchen floor, soon there's a whole line of ants carting crumbs away. How did that first ant tell the others to come and get it?

The first ant was out searching for food. When she (the worker ants are always female) found some, she put down an invisible trail—a path of chemicals that only ants from the finder ant's nest could follow. These chemical signals are called *pheromones* (FAIR-o-moans). Pheromones work in the dark, under ground, or under water. Almost nothing stands in their way. Some last only a few minutes; others last hours, days, or even weeks. Some pheromones send alarms that warn of danger, some are left by animals looking for mates, and some are trail markers. Each species of animal has its own personal pheromone. For example, a carpenter ant cannot follow the trail of a fire ant or a black household ant.

On her way back to the nest, the ant that found the crumbs stopped every few inches to touch the tip of her abdomen to the ground to leave a drop of pheromone. The other worker ants could smell or taste the chemical and followed her trail to the food. As each ant returned to the nest, she also left drops of the chemical message.

If a fire ant finds a bit of food too big to carry, she walks slowly back to the nest to get help. Every few inches along the way, her stinger appears from the end of her abdomen, and she draws the tip of that stinger lightly over the ground. As she does, the pheromone flows down from a small sac called Dufour's gland. The amount of pheromone she leaves is also part of the message. The better the new food supply is, the more pheromone she deposits.

Along with the pheromone that marks a trail to food, ants have a pheromone that can send a chemical alarm to warn of danger, and another to signal death. When an ant dies, its body releases a pheromone that tells the worker ants to pick up the dead body and dump it on the garbage pile outside the nest. To test this behavior, some scientists painted live ants with the death pheromone. Sure enough, the worker ants picked up the painted ants and dumped them outside. When the "dead" painted ants—who were really alive and well—hurried back to the nest, they were picked up and tossed on the pile again and again. Even though the worker ants must have seen and felt the struggles of the live ants, they were programmed to follow the chemical message that told them to get those dead ants out of there.

Scientists have learned how to kill or catch insects by using an insect's own pheromone instead of pesticides. Male Japanese beetles are lured into traps that have been baited with the female beetles' pheromone. The males can't help themselves. An inborn action, or instinct, makes them follow the chemical signal to find a mate. Mosquitoes, gypsy moths, cockroaches, and many other insects are now caught in traps baited by chemical signals of their own species.

Wolves mark the boundaries of their land with pheromones to make sure no other pack moves into that territory. They urinate on trees, shrubs, and rocks. An-

Pheromone-baited traps lure Japanese beetles

other wolf trotting past gets the pheromone message in the urine as surely as we'd understand a sign that read, "Keep out." Dogs do the same thing.

A cat rubs its head against furniture and door frames to leave a pheromone that marks the house as its own territory, even though people happen to live there, too. Male cats spray a liquid that tells other cats they've been there. It apparently smells good to a female cat, but it's not an odor people like at all. All the big cats—lions, tigers, cheetahs, jaguars, mountain lions—leave chemical messages to mark their territory, too.

Beavers leave their pheromone on plops of mud that one naturalist calls "mudpie telegrams." One sniff and other beavers can read the messages from these markers.

Darting through fields and woods, deer might easily get separated from one another. But they stay in touch with pheromone signs. The black-tailed deer, for example, leaves a message whenever it lies down or rubs its head against a tree. The pheromones are made by glands on the deer's hind legs, on its tail, between its hooves, and on its forehead. A fawn can find its mother, a male can find a female, and a stray deer can find the herd by sniffing these chemical signals.

Not all chemical messages are invisible, however—and not all chemical messages are relayed by pheromones.

Some animals are *bioluminescent* (bio-loom-in-ESS-ent). *Bio* means "life," and *luminescent* means "lighting up," so a bioluminescent creature is actually a living light. On summer nights, fireflies blink their signals. Sometimes called lightning bugs, fireflies are actually beetles. The light, which glows through a "window" in the rear segment of the firefly's abdomen, is made from a substance called *luciferin* (loo-SIF-er-in).

Most of the two thousand species of fireflies live in the tropics. About fifty kinds of fireflies live in the United States

Beavers "read" pheromone messages

 11

and Canada. Each species sends its own specific mating signal, which never changes. A male, for example, may send two flashes of orange light, 1½ seconds apart. A female of the same species answers with that same pattern 1 second later. Her signal tells the male that she recognizes his code, that she is one of his species. Another kind of firefly flashes an orange light when it flies and a green light when it's on the ground. After fireflies mate, the female's light goes out, and she lays her eggs in the ground. Some of the tiny larvae growing inside the eggs glow even before they hatch. (These larvae are sometimes called *glowworms*.) Once in a while, a toad or lizard eats so many fireflies that it, too, seems to glow like a night-light.

Along the shore of an island in Southeast Asia, one kind of firefly does the work of a lighthouse. There, thousands of fireflies live in mangrove trees close to the water's edge. Every night, when they flash their signals in the same steady rhythm, the light is so strong and constant that ships at sea can use it as a marker to steer a safe course.

2
DANCING BEES

A honeybee returns to her hive

When a honeybee discovers a rich supply of nectar, it flies back to the hive to tell the other bees exactly where the food is. The bee even tells them what kind it is, and how good it is. How can an insect with a brain no bigger than a grass seed describe all this information?

Dr. Karl von Frisch was the first person to find out. He put a dot of red dye on a worker bee and watched as she flew off and returned to the hive. (Worker bees are always female.) As he watched thousands of bees, Dr. von Frisch discovered how they sent their messages. They danced!

He called it the "waggle dance." The pattern of a bee's dance is a figure eight. She repeats it over and over again as her sister bees watch. The most important part of the dance is the straight run through the middle of the figure eight.

That shows the direction from the hive to the food. If the bee is dancing outside the hive on a flat surface, she lines up with the sun, then turns to point toward the food. If the bee is inside, on the wall of the dark hive, her head points up, as if the sun were overhead. Then she turns right or left to show where the food is.

As she runs through the figure eight, the bee waggles her head and tail from side to side. The farther away the food is, the faster she dances. Different kinds

Worker bees gather to watch the "waggle dancer"

of bees have different waggle signals. For German honeybees, one waggle means the food is about fifty yards away. Italian bees, which are favored by beekeepers in the United States, use one waggle to mean about twenty-five yards.

As she dances, the bee's wings vibrate so fast that they buzz. The other worker bees touch the dancer with their antennae to feel the vibrations. They also sample a drop of the nectar she has found. In a few minutes, the first bees to figure out where the food is fly away. Then the others move up to touch the dancer bee, and they leave the hive as soon as they know the directions, too. Before each bee flies off, she lines up facing the sun and turns in the direction that the waggle dancer pointed.

The information given by a dancing bee is so accurate that scientists can follow the bee's directions and find the same flowers.

In 1988, a team of scientists from Denmark and Germany built a tiny electronic robot honeybee that was run by a computer. The robot bee was designed to "talk" to a hive full of bees and give them instructions to fly to a specific spot. The robot doesn't look much like a real bee, but it doesn't have to, because a bee hive is dark. All the robot has to do is send signals the bees can understand—and offer a sample of the food.

Before the scientists could test the robot, they had to get real bees to taste the peppermint-scented sugar water they would use as bait. They put a dish of sugar water almost a mile away from a hive, and let a worker bee from that hive taste it. (They had marked the worker bee so they could recognize her.) When the worker bee flew back to the hive, she danced and gave samples of the food, and almost three hundred bees followed her instructions. They found the peppermint-scented sugar water a mile away.

The next step was to program the robot bee to dance the directions to the sugar water, which had been moved to

The robot bee gives directions

a new spot. In the hive, the bees gathered around and paid attention to the robot bee. But could they follow the robot's directions? That was the big test. When the dancing robot bee buzzed and waggled and gave samples of the food (the scientists released a drop of the sugar water through a tiny brass tube above the robot's head), almost a hundred bees found the sugar water. The robot wasn't quite as successful as the real bee—but the robot was obviously working.

Then they tried some other experiments. For example, when the robot gave samples but didn't dance, only ten bees found the food. When the robot danced but didn't give samples, or when it danced and gave samples but didn't whir its wings, very few bees found their way to the sugar water. Finally the scientists knew that the bees needed the whole message—the waggle dance, the whirring wings, and a taste of the food.

The keepers of the robot bee can hardly wait to find out what else it will tell them. They are ready for surprises.

3
BODY LANGUAGE

By rolling over, a dog sends a message to its owner

You're walking down the street when suddenly you see a big dog in a yard two houses away. Is it a fierce watchdog or just a friendly old mutt? It isn't hard to tell the difference if you can "read" the dog's body language. If the dog bares its teeth and growls, you'd be wise to stay away, but if it crouches low and wags its tail, you can be pretty sure it's friendly.

We use body language to communicate every day. If your mother stares down at you with a frown on her face and her hands on her hips, you can read her message. Before she says one word, you know you're in trouble. But when she reaches over to hug you, it's easy to understand that nice message, too. Whether or not we speak to someone, we're communicating as we smile, frown, point, wave, shake hands, shrug, hug, or turn away.

Body language not only sends signals between animals of the same kind— dog to dog, lion to lion, or human to human, for example—it can also be a means of communication between different kinds of animals—for example, between dogs and humans, or cats and birds.

Wolves greet others in their packs with wagging tails. It's easy to tell which wolf is the leader, because all the other wolves bow their heads and crouch before him. Sometimes a dog greets its owner with such tail wagging that its whole body seems to wag. It may roll over, belly up, to have its tummy scratched. But the dog isn't being cute. Like the wolves, the dog is sending a message to its "leader." Its actions are saying, "I know you're the boss; I'll do anything for you, even leave myself unprotected like this."

If you meet a hissing cat with its back arched and its tail straight up, you know it's ready to fight if it has to. But if a cat rubs against your leg and purrs, you know its message is friendly. Birds can also read the body language of a cat. If the cat is sprawled on the grass in a patch of sun under the bird feeder, the birds will often continue to eat. But if that cat stalks and crouches, ready to pounce, the birds usually fly away.

There's no need to fear a skunk if you pay attention to the signals it sends before it sprays. A cornered skunk will turn its back, raise its fluffy tail, and stamp its dainty feet to warn you it means business. As long as the tip of the skunk's tail droops a little, you're safe. But when the skunk's tail flies straight up, it's too late— the skunk is going to spray.

Some animals use body language to attract a mate. The peacock spreads his shimmering tail into a five-foot fan as he struts past the peahens. The message he's sending may be something like "Look at me; I'm the best." A male pigeon also struts, but he drags his tail feathers on the ground and puffs out his chest. Prairie chickens gather like people at a square dance. Each male fluffs up his feathers as he shuffles his feet and runs back and forth, holding his neck stiff and his beak pointed down. The females stand around and watch for a while, until each one finally chooses a dancer for her mate.

Some silent signals are harder to figure out than others. One question that has so far stumped scientists is how a school of fish or a flock of birds can stay so close together that they seem to turn at the same instant, as though they're all attached. Who sends the message that they are suddenly going to turn right or left? Is it one leader? If so, then who becomes the leader when they turn to fly or swim in the opposite direction? How can a flock of ten thousand starlings make a quick turn and never crash into one another? How can a million minnows swimming in one direction suddenly dart off together when they are threatened by a big fish? We haven't learned to read the body language of all animals yet, and maybe we never will.

When space scientists opened the capsule of a U.S. *Mercury* rocket that had just returned from an eight-hour flight, there was Ham, the first chimpanzee astronaut. His lips were pulled back in a wide, toothy "smile." Everyone cheered, and the photographers snapped pictures that were printed in newspapers around the world. Headlines said that Ham was smiling because he loved his space flight.

But Ham's was not a happy face. It

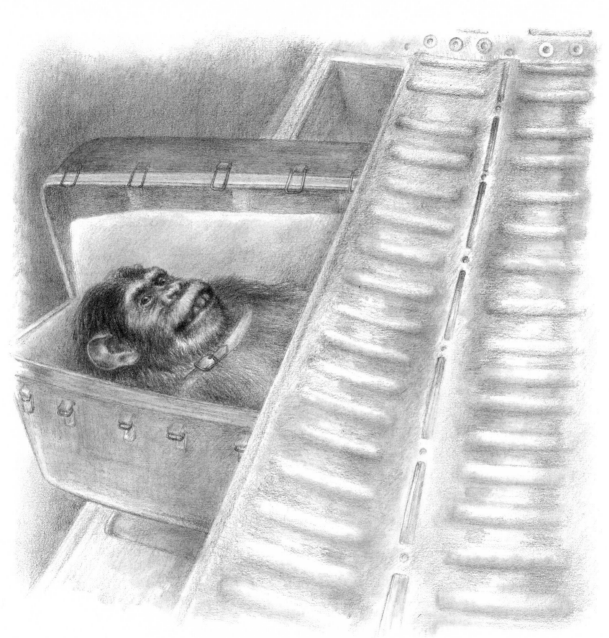

Ham "smiles" for the photographers

was the chimpanzee's look of fear or anger. Ham's "play" face would have been an open-mouthed, relaxed grin, with no teeth showing. Just because we smile and show our teeth when we're happy, we can't assume that other animals do, too. That kind of mistake even has a scientific name. It's called *anthropomorphism* (an-throw-po-MORE-fizm). *Anthropo* means "human," and *morphic* means "form." The word means "thinking of animals as though they were human." But, of course, they aren't, and we must try to pay as much attention to the motions, tail flips, and changing faces of animals as we do to our own language.

4
BARKS, CHIRPS, AND MELODIES

A young vervet monkey calls out a warning

As the sun rose over the African plains, a vervet monkey stretched and yawned. Silently he swung through the branches of a baobob tree and dropped to the ground. A shadow passed overhead, and the monkey froze. An eagle was circling! The monkey gave the alarm, a loud chuckle that warned—eagle! The other monkeys looked up and then scrambled for cover in dense thickets nearby. An eagle could grab a monkey out in the open, or even in a tree, but not so easily in the bushes.

Their warning calls have made vervet monkeys famous among scientists who study animal communication. If a vervet monkey sees a leopard, its call is a loud bark that sends the other monkeys running for the treetops. Leopards can climb trees, but not fast enough to grab a monkey there. Leopards are more likely to get food if they lie in wait in the grass to ambush monkeys passing by. The monkeys have learned this, so they head for high branches. If the troop hears a loud, chittering call, all the monkeys stand on their hind legs and look around for a dangerous snake, especially a python. Another call alerts them to baboons, who sometimes grab young monkeys. A different cry goes out when they see the enemy they fear the most— a human being.

Scientists wanted to know if the monkeys really understood each differ-

ent warning, so they recorded the calls when they could also see what had frightened the monkeys. If they saw an eagle fly over, they recorded the monkeys' calls. Later, when there were no dangerous animals in sight, they played back the alarm calls through a loudspeaker in the bushes.

When the eagle alarm was played, the monkeys looked up and headed for the bushes. The leopard call sent the monkeys into the trees. Because the monkeys reacted to the recorded alarm calls, even though no leopard or eagle or snake was in sight, the scientists knew that the monkeys understood each call as clearly as humans would understand a word. Each call meant a specific danger to them.

Next the scientists wanted to find out if the monkeys learned the alarm calls or if the calls were something they were born knowing. The answer is that the calls seem to be partly learned and partly inborn. Baby vervet monkeys holler out alarms for all kinds of things. They give snake alarms when they see plodding tortoises or twisted vines. They give leopard alarms for warthogs and zebras. One tiny monkey screamed a hawk alarm when it saw a flying leaf.

At first they make mistakes, but baby monkeys know enough to give hawk or eagle alarms for things in the air, and leopard alarms for animals that walk on four legs, and snake alarms for things on the ground. It seems as though they have basic alarm information from birth, but they have to learn the specifics from the grownups. If a baby gives a leopard alarm for a warthog passing by, the adults glance up. When they see that it's a harmless animal, the adults do nothing. But if the adults do see a leopard, they give the leopard alarm, too. It's as though the

A harmless warthog is no cause for alarm

grownups were telling the babies, "Don't worry; it's only a warthog"—or "That was the right call; it really is a leopard; head for the treetops." After a few weeks, the young monkeys don't need to check with the grownups anymore.

Hardly an animal on earth doesn't make some sound. But seldom are the sounds just noise. Most are a matter of life or death.

All birds give simple alarm and warning calls. They give different calls when they're about to take flight, or when they're hurt, or when they're getting in touch with birds separated from the flock.

Calls can also keep a mother in touch with her babies. Ducks use an "assembly" call to gather the babies close. Baby ducks give a "contentment" call when they are safe with their mother. They even start this call while they are still in the eggs. And they give a "distress" call when separated from their mother or the rest of the ducklings.

For years scientists wondered why some birds sing their dawn chorus each spring, because a singing bird gives away its position to a predator. A long song can be dangerous. It's the same as saying, "Here I am." It's one thing to give a chink or tweet that alerts other birds to danger, but a lot of energy goes into the long songs that are sung alone. They must be worth the risk.

Ninety-five percent of the dawn chorus singers are male birds. The males get back to their summer territory first, to scout around for a good place to build a nest before the females arrive. There's a lot of competition for the safest spots, but in about two weeks each male bird has staked his claim. That's when the singing begins. The robin's cheery "cheeriup, cheerily, cheeriup" is his way of telling other robins to stay out, he got there first.

Scientists wondered if birds learned their songs or if they were inborn. They found out that a songbird is born know-

A female robin joins her mate in the territory he has claimed

ing the general pattern of its family's song, but it also learns parts of it. Before it is seven weeks old, the bird must hear its family song or it will never really know all the notes. A bird raised alone can only make a general singsongy sound.

After a young male bird has heard another bird of the same species sing his family song, he practices and practices as he listens to his own voice. Later, he begins to invent a few changes. He improvises. The goldfinch has a long warbling song that's repeated over and over for half a minute or more. The older a goldfinch gets, the more extra warbles he sings. Canaries tend to make more variations in their songs as they get older, too.

Scientists were surprised to find that one species of bird may sing different songs in different parts of the country. The male wrens in Oregon, for example, sing thirty different songs, but in New York State, they sing only two. Long-billed marsh wrens that live in the West have about one hundred fifty different songs, but in the East they have fifty. What makes the difference? Does something in the environment cause birds to sing more or less? Perhaps someday we'll learn the answers to these questions.

5
ECHOES IN THE DARK

A mother bat finds her offspring among hundreds of babies

"Blind as a bat," people used to say, but bats aren't blind at all. They can see in daylight. "Bats get tangled in your hair," people said. But bats are very skilled at finding their way in the dark. In one experiment, they flew at forty miles an hour through a maze of fine wires crisscrossing a darkened room and never touched a wire.

Bats find their way by *echolocation*.

They send out sounds that echo back from walls, trees, other bats, and even from the tiniest insects. Those echoes help them locate various objects. We humans have reinvented echolocation and call it *sonar.* (The name stands for *so*und *na*vigation *r*anging.) Submarines use sonar to find their way in deep water.

A constant stream of sound goes out through a bat's nostrils. Its nose is surrounded by a complicated fold of skin called the *noseleaf.* Noseleaves are important because they focus the outgoing sounds. As the sounds bounce off objects and echo back, they are picked up by the bat's ears. All these sounds are *ultrasonic,* meaning they are pitched *above* the level of sound humans can hear. We can hear ultrasounds only when they are recorded and then played back at very slow speeds.

When a bat is just cruising through the air, it may send out as few as 5 or as many as 20 sounds each second. But as it approaches a landing, or gets near a moth, for example, it might send out anywhere from 50 to 200 sounds a second. In this way, it can gather more detailed information about the landing surface or the moth. Horseshoe bats of Africa hang upside down from their roosts and scan the air with a beam of ultrasonic sounds, like a ground-to-air missile-detecting radar system. If an insect flies across the scanning beam, the bat flies out and catches it.

Bats use their echolocation not only to hunt but also to send information to other bats. A bat's message might tell what species it is, where it is going, or if it is chasing insects. But the most important messages may be sent by mother bats to their babies. Imagine a million mother bats looking for their own infants among two or three million screaming baby bats hanging from a cave roof. At one time, it was thought that any bat mother fed any baby, but that has been proven false.

A mother bat sends out her echo-

Echolocation helps bats zero in on their prey

location call as she flies into the cave, and the baby answers with its own call. Then the mother sends a very different double-note call, which the baby answers again and again until the mother finds the general area where she left the baby hanging upside down. When she's narrowed the choice down to a few hundred babies in one part of the cave, she keeps sending and following calls until she's close enough to recognize the smell of her own baby.

31

Like bats, dolphins use ultrasonic echolocation to hunt in the dark. They also make a lot of noises, even though they have no vocal cords. Dolphins squeak, moan, whistle, chirp, chuckle, bark, and rattle. They can even give a "Bronx cheer," also known as a "raspberry." All these sounds come through the blowhole in the top of the head. But sonar clicks are sent out from the bulge on the dolphin's forehead, which is called the *melon*. The echoes that bounce back from an object are picked up as vibrations in the dolphin's hollow lower jaw. From there, they travel to the middle ear.

When a dolphin is just cruising through the ocean looking for food, it sends out clicks at a rate of perhaps 10 each second. But as the dolphin gets about six feet from its target, the clicks speed up to 400 each second. We can't hear the individual clicks, but when a whole train of these high-speed clicks pulse together, it sounds to human ears like rusty hinges opening or the whine of machinery.

It's amazing that dolphins can understand their messages, because the ocean is not a quiet place. Sound travels faster and farther under water than it does in the air. Oysters clack, shrimp holler, and toadfish bleat like foghorns. And among the calls of hundreds of other fish and mammals are the roars of engines in passing ships. While one dolphin is sending a message, it might be getting messages from a dozen other dolphins. But somehow the dolphin's brain can sort it out.

No one knows what dolphins are saying to one another, of course. Their communications are still mysterious. At one aquarium, a pair of bottlenose dolphins were placed in tanks side by side. They couldn't see each other, but they could hear. The female dolphin was taught to push paddles in order to get a reward of food. The male dolphin had paddles in his tank, too, but he was not

Bottlenose dolphins communicate through ultrasonic echolocation

trained to use them. Imagine how surprised the trainers were to find that the male dolphin had learned to push the right paddles anyway. While the female dolphin was being trained, both dolphins had kept up a constant stream of whistles, squeaks, and rusty-hinge noises. Was the female "telling" the male how to push the paddles in order to get some fish? It was either that or the male dolphin trained himself, which would be remarkable, too.

At sea, a hundred or more dolphins usually line up side by side to hunt. Each one sends out its ultrasonic sounds until they echo back from a school of fish. Their strong sonar can stun or even kill fish, so dolphins must use echolocation "manners." Such manners have been seen in captive dolphins. If one dolphin in a tank crosses in front of another, the dolphin using its sonar stops sending signals and turns its head away. It goes back to using sonar only after the other dolphin is out of the way. Echolocation manners must be especially important in a school of hundreds of dolphins. It may be one reason why dolphins stay in formation most of the time. From hunting in a line side by side, they move into a circle to attack a school of fish, and all the dolphins dive at once. Maybe their ultrasonic signals keep them in step, like synchronized swimmers.

6
MESSAGES BY THE MILE

Fin whales are the second-largest animals in the world

F in whales swim fast and travel alone, but they stay in touch with other fin whales hundreds of miles away. You might think the world's second-largest animal (only the blue whale is larger) would have the loudest voice, but we can't hear even a trace of the fin whale's long-distance song. Its sound is *infrasonic*, meaning it is *below* the level humans can hear. The

35

rumblings of earthquakes, volcanoes, and severe thunderstorms are also infrasonic as they are building. We may feel them before they erupt, but we don't hear them. Divers swimming near big whales say they can feel the sound tingle right through their bodies. In the days before the churning engines of big ships filled the oceans with noise, the songs of fin whales may have carried for two or three thousand miles.

How whales make their sounds is still a mystery. They have no vocal cords. As one scientist put it, whales have a lot of complicated "plumbing" in their heads, and we don't know how it all works. Whales often sing near canyons on the ocean bottoms. Sounds echo from these deep hollows and trenches. Musicians say the songs sound as if they've been amplified in a recording studio.

Dr. Roger Payne and Dr. Katherine Payne, a husband-and-wife team, studied whale songs for twenty years. They began by recording the sounds made by humpback whales feeding in the cold waters of the Arctic and Antarctic oceans in the spring. They could hear long, low rumbles, shrill whistles, grunts, eerie groans, and high squeaks like a door opening on a rusty hinge (much like the sounds of the dolphins). Some noises were used when whales met. Perhaps they were asking, "Who are you?" or warning others to stay away; perhaps the sounds were simply a form of greeting. All the "conversations" were short.

It wasn't until the humpback whales had migrated to breeding grounds in warm seas—around Hawaii, California, Bermuda, or Africa—that the Paynes heard the male humpback's beautiful, long melody. The humpback sings this song only when he is alone. His tune is the most complicated of all animal songs, with many notes in different patterns. Most humpback songs last an hour or two, interrupted only when the whale comes up for air. But one scientist taped a song that went on for more than twenty-

Humpback songs are recorded by a diver

two hours. The whale was still singing when the scientist got tired and packed up his equipment to go home.

The humpback's songs change each season. At the beginning of the spring migration, the males in one part of the ocean pick up the old melody and begin to make changes in it. They improvise. The song may drop in pitch, or one part may be speeded up while another slows down. As soon as one whale sings a new song, the other whales learn it. We depend on rhymes and repeating choruses to help us remember long songs and poems. Whales do, too. They repeat rhythms and patterns of notes.

Whales from the Pacific Ocean sing a different song from those in the Atlantic. In twenty years of study, the North Atlantic humpbacks have never gone back to an old version of a song after they have changed it. Does an old song go out of style? Is it a message they no longer need? Are they now telling a "story" of things that happened during the most recent migration? Nobody knows.

Some years after the whale studies, Dr. Katherine Payne was watching a group of elephants at the Washington Park Zoo, in Portland, Oregon. The elephants were separated by thick concrete walls, but they called back and forth with their usual trumpetings, snorts, barks, and rumbles. For centuries, people who lived near elephants have heard such rumblings. Some claimed it was only the elephants' stomachs digesting food. But at the zoo that day, Dr. Payne felt a strange throbbing in the air every ten or fifteen seconds.

Later, back in her office at Cornell University, she kept thinking about that feeling. It reminded her of when she was a young girl, singing in the church choir. She had felt the same throbbing from the lowest notes of the big pipe organ. It also felt like the vibrations from the whales' infrasonic songs. Could the elephants be sending infrasonic messages?

Infrasonic calls would explain how herds stay in touch, even though they are separated by thick forests. Infrasonic communication might also help explain some of the elephants' behavior. For example, a group of grandmother and mother elephants traveling with babies, aunts, and baby-sitters sometimes stops suddenly. For a minute or two, they stand still as statues, with their ears fanned out. Then, just as suddenly, they change direction and march away. How do two or three groups of elephants manage to arrive at a waterhole at the same time? They run from different directions and greet each other as old friends. How does a male elephant traveling alone find a fe-

Elephants listen for infrasonic messages

male for a mate? If we found that elephants sent infrasonic messages, that would answer a lot of our questions.

Dr. Payne and her team went back to the zoo with recording equipment that could pick up the sounds we can't hear. When the tapes were played back at higher speed, the sounds were clear. There's a spot on an elephant's forehead that trembles when the animal makes the deep rumbling or purring sounds that we hear. But whenever the taping equipment registered the low-level "silent" sounds, the elephant's forehead also fluttered. Dr. Payne knew she was right. The elephant's secret language wasn't secret anymore. Like fin whales, elephants communicated with infrasound.

7
CONVERSATIONS
WITH GREAT APES

Washoe makes the sign for "I"

Washoe, a chimpanzee, was the first animal to point to herself and say, "I." Scientists had argued for centuries about whether or not animals knew who they were. Were they just machines that went through the motions of living by instinct? Or did they really know what they were doing? Washoe answered those questions, for chimpanzees, at least.

Washoe grew up in a trailer in Allen and Beatrice Gardner's backyard in Nevada. In 1966, the Gardners began to teach the young chimp American Sign Language, also known as Ameslan, which is used by many deaf people. It is not English but rather a combination of gestures and hand motions that mean words and phrases.

At first Washoe made simple signs, such as those for *hat, out, come,* and *ball.* A lot of scientists thought that wasn't so amazing, because she was just imitating her trainers. But all baby animals learn by imitation. Human babies certainly do. We hold up a ball and say to the baby, "Ball." Pretty soon the baby learns to call that round thing a ball.

By the time she was five years old, Washoe knew 150 signs. She could tell the Gardners, "You me go out," for example. She knew the difference between "You tickle me" and "I tickle you." (She loved to be tickled.)

Once in a while Washoe invented signs. Before she ate, Washoe had to put on a bib. The gesture the Gardners used for the word *bib* was the Ameslan gesture for "wiper." Washoe was supposed to touch her mouth with five fingers in a wiping motion. But Washoe forgot, so instead she drew the outline of a bib on her chest. The Gardners told her that was wrong. Imagine their surprise when they discovered that Washoe's sign for bib was the right one in Ameslan!

Lucy is another chimpanzee who learned to "talk" to humans in American Sign Language. When she didn't know the names for what she saw, she used combinations of words she did know. She called swans "water birds"; watermelon was "candy drink."

Koko is a gorilla who did the same thing. She called a mask an "eye hat" and a ring a "finger bracelet." A frozen banana was a "fruit lollipop," and a lemon was a "dirty orange." "Dirty" was Koko's word for anything she didn't like, and she didn't like lemons.

Koko signs "cat" by drawing two fingers across her cheek

Of all the great apes that took part in these experiments, Koko is the most famous. She was the first animal to tell us how she felt. She really surprised everyone when she made jokes, rhymed words, and insulted people. Her full name is Hanabi-Ko, which is Japanese for "Fireworks Child." Koko was born on the Fourth of July in 1971, and a year later she went to live with Dr. Francine (Penny) Patterson.

Koko had never lived in the wild with a gorilla family. She may not have known all the calls wild gorillas used, but she gave the same gentle *naoom naoom* grunts of contentment that a wild gorilla baby does. And no one had to teach her how to thump her chest to warn intruders or let out a whoop-bark, which is a wild gorilla's call of alarm. Many of Koko's sounds and gestures were inborn—she didn't have to learn them. But what she did learn surprised everyone, even Dr. Patterson, who was certain that Koko could "talk" to her.

Some scientists weren't sure that Koko really knew what she was doing. But when one scientist asked Koko in sign language if she was a person or a gorilla, Koko signed back, "Fine animal gorilla."

Koko has always loved to have someone read to her. She still spends hours looking at picture books, especially *The Three Little Kittens* and *Puss in Boots*. She makes the sign for cat by drawing two fingers across her cheek like whiskers.

Before Koko's birthday one year, someone showed her three real kittens. Koko looked them over carefully and finally chose one that had no tail. "Love that," Koko signed. And she named the kitten All Ball.

Dr. Patterson drew a picture of a cat on Koko's birthday cake. She asked Koko, "What did I draw?" Koko signed, "Ball. Koko love visit Ball." Koko acted like a child with a pet. She would never hurt the kitten. But if All Ball nipped her, Koko would always sign, "Obnoxious." And then later she'd sign, "Soft good cat cat." Koko carried All Ball on her back the way a good gorilla mother carries her baby. And she cuddled the kitten gently in her arms.

When All Ball was killed in an accident, Koko cried. She kept signing "cat" and "All Ball." Finally Dr. Patterson gave Koko a doll, hoping it would make her happy. But Koko tossed the doll aside and signed, "That stink."

Scientists continue to ask, "What is language?" and "Do apes really talk?" Of course, Koko and Washoe and Lucy and the others don't use our language. No matter how hard they try, chimpanzees and gorillas can never talk as we do. They don't have the same kind of vocal cords. But does that matter? They speak to us in their own way. For the first time, there is real communication between humans and other animals. It's a wonderful gift.

What more would they ask us if they could? What more would they tell us if they could?

Koko named her tailless kitten All Ball

INDEX